WHAT'S IN YOUR SODA?

Jaclyn Sullivan

PowerKiDS press™

New York

To Paul, Kim, and Miranda, my favorite Peppers

Published in 2012 by The Rosen Publishing Group, Inc.
29 East 21st Street, New York, NY 10010

First Edition

Editor: Sara Antill
Book Design: Greg Tucker

Photo Credits: Cover, pp. 4, 10, 11, 14, 15 Shutterstock.com; p. 5 Digital Vision/Thinkstock; p. 6 Petrified Collection/The Image Bank/Getty Images; pp. 7, 8, 17, 19 (bottom) iStockphoto/Thinkstock; pp. 9, 12, 13 (bottom) Hemera/Thinkstock; p. 13 (top) Photodisc/Thinkstock; p. 18 Creatas Images/Creatas/Thinkstock; p. 19 (top) BananaStock/Thinkstock; p. 20 Jupiterimages/Polka Dot/Thinkstock; p. 21 (top) Jupiterimages/Brand X Pictures/Thinkstock; p. 21 (bottom) Mario Tama/Getty Images; p. 22 George Doyle/Stockbyte/Thinkstock.

Library of Congress Cataloging-in-Publication Data

Sullivan, Jaclyn.
  What's in your soda? / by Jaclyn Sullivan. — 1st ed.
      p. cm. — (What's in your fast food)
  ISBN 978-1-4488-6210-8 (library binding) — ISBN 978-1-4488-6379-2 (pbk.) —
ISBN 978-1-4488-6380-8 (6-pack)
  1. Soft drinks—Juvenile literature. 2. Nutrition—Juvenile literature. 3. Convenience foods—Juvenile literature. I. Title. II. Series.
  TP630.S85 2012
  641.2'6—dc23

2011032105

Manufactured in the United States of America

CPSIA Compliance Information: Batch #WW12PK: For Further Information contact Rosen Publishing, New York, New York at 1-800-237-9932

Contents

Soda Everywhere!

Soda is often sold in bottles and cans.

If you are like many people, you probably like a sweet, fizzy drink called soda. You can find soda at restaurants, grocery stores, and gas stations. People drink soda at the movies and at sports games. There are even vending machines that sell only soda. Sometimes it seems that soda is everywhere!

You might think that soda is a good drink choice for you because it is so

This boy is drinking a glass of soda with his dinner. Drinking soda with meals can add a lot of extra sugar to your diet.

easy to find. You have probably seen a lot of adults drinking soda, too. Drinking soda once in a while will not make you sick. However, soda is generally not a healthy choice. Learning what is in soda will help you understand why.

Soda Beginnings

For thousands of years, people believed that drinking the fizzy **mineral water** from natural springs could cure sicknesses. In 1767, a British scientist named Joseph Priestley figured out how

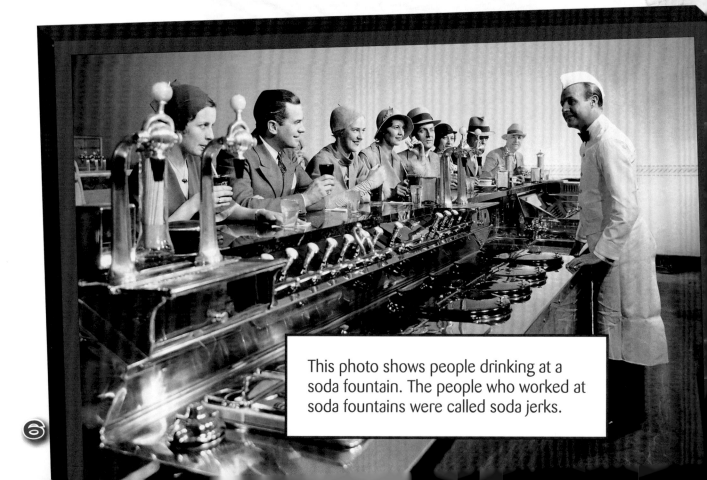

This photo shows people drinking at a soda fountain. The people who worked at soda fountains were called soda jerks.

to use a gas called **carbon dioxide** to make bubbles in water. His invention, called soda water, looked and tasted a lot like natural mineral water.

Throughout the 1800s, inventors created new machines that could make soda water very quickly. Special stores called soda fountains used the machines to make and sell soda. They added sugary **syrups** to give the soda water different flavors. People thought that this new drink was as healthy as mineral water.

The amount of soda people drink has gone up a lot in the last 100 years. Today, the average American drinks more than 575 cans of soda every year!

Bubbles and Fizz

Early bottle caps needed to be removed with a bottle opener. Today, many bottle caps can be removed by twisting them off.

For a long time, people could drink soda only at soda fountains. Then, in 1892, a man named William Painter invented a bottle cap that could keep carbon dioxide trapped in glass bottles. This was the key to bottling soda so people could drink it at home.

Do you know that hissing noise you hear when you first open a can or bottle of soda? That sound comes from the

You can see the bubbles of carbon dioxide as they rise to the top of this glass of soda. When most of the carbon dioxide has escaped, the soda will have very little fizz.

carbon dioxide in soda. When **carbonated** water is put under pressure, the carbon dioxide is trapped. When you open a bottle or can of soda, the carbon dioxide is able to escape.

How Is Soda Made?

This woman is cutting grapes from a vine. Grapes and other fruit can be used to make juices or flavored teas. Most sodas do not have any real fruit in them, though.

Most soda is made in big factories called bottling plants. There, water is mixed with **sweeteners** and **artificial**, or man-made, flavors. Carbon dioxide is added to the mixture to give it its fizz. The soda is then put into bottles and cans.

Food scientists create artificial flavors in labs. They can make flavors that taste like almost anything, even fruits such as oranges or lemons. Just because some

These plastic bottles are about to be filled with soda. They will then be packaged and shipped to stores where they can be sold.

sodas taste like they have fruit in them does not mean they are healthy, though. Real fruit has **vitamins** and **nutrients** that are good for you. Artificial flavors do not have these vitamins and nutrients.

High-Fructose Corn Syrup

Did you know that the sweetener in most sodas is made from corn? This type of sugar is called **high-fructose corn syrup**. High-fructose corn syrup is much sweeter and less expensive to use than other types of sugar.

Some people believe that high-fructose corn syrup is not harmful to our bodies. However, high-fructose

Table sugar is made up of fructose and glucose. Most high-fructose corn syrup does not have more fructose than table sugar. It is called high-fructose corn syrup because it has more fructose than regular corn syrup.

corn syrup has a lot of empty **calories**. Calories measure the energy in food. Empty calories come from foods with a lot of fat or sugar and very few nutrients. Eating or drinking too many calories can make us gain weight.

FAST-FOOD FACTS

Americans eat and drink twice the amount of sugar they did 30 years ago. Each person eats or drinks about 22 teaspoons of sugar every day!

Diet Soda

A 2010 study by scientists at the University of Texas Health Science Center showed that people who drank diet soda gained more fat around their waists than people who did not drink any soda.

Since regular sodas have a lot of empty calories, is diet soda a better drink choice? Instead of sugars, diet sodas use artificial sweeteners that have fewer or no calories. Eating and drinking fewer calories can help people lose weight.

Just having fewer calories does not mean diet sodas are healthy, though. In fact, some scientists think that artificial sweeteners might make some people gain

A study in the 1970s found that saccharine, a sweetener in some diet sodas, caused a certain type of cancer in lab rats. However, in the 2000s, it was shown that saccharine did not cause the same kind of sickness in people.

even more weight. When we taste something sweet, our bodies expect to get calories. Artificial sweeteners with no calories may affect the way our brains work and cause us to eat more sugary foods.

Nutrition Facts

Serving Size 1 can
Servings Per Container: 1

Amount Per Serving

Calories 140

	% Daily Value *
	0%
Total Fat 0g	2%
Sodium 45mg	13%
Total Carbohydrate 39g	
Sugar 39g	0%
Protein 0g	

Vitamin A 0%	•	Vitamin C 0%
Calcium 0%	•	Iron 0%

*Percent Daily Values are based on a 2,000 calorie diet. Your daily values may be higher or lower depending on your calorie needs.

	Calories	2,000	2,500
Total Fat	Less than	65g	80g
Sat Fat	Less than	20g	25g
Cholesterol	Less than	300mg	300mg
Sodium	Less than	300mg	300mg
Total Carbohydrate		300g	375g
Dietary Fiber		25g	30g

Calories per gram:
Fat 9 • Carbohydrate 4 • Protein 4

Reading labels can help you learn if a drink is healthy. You can check soda labels on the backs of bottles or cans. The label will tell you how many calories and how much sugar are in your soda.

You can also learn about the **ingredients** in soda by reading labels. Ingredients are all of the things in soda that make it a soda! The ingredients are listed in order of how much of

This is an example of a label on a can of soda. This soda would not provide any of the vitamin A or vitamin C that you need in a day to stay healthy.

Drinking sodas made with artificial sweeteners instead of sugars might be better for people with a sickness called diabetes. People with diabetes have to be very careful about how much sugar they eat and drink.

each ingredient there is in the soda from most to least. The ingredient list will tell you if your soda is made with high-fructose corn syrup or an artificial sweetener.

Soda Dangers

Today, most people know that soda is not as healthy as water. However, many people believe that there is nothing wrong with drinking a lot of soda. Scientists have proved, though, that there are some things in soda that will hurt our bodies if we drink too much.

Soda can cause our bones to become softer, which means they could break more easily. The sugars in soda

Brushing your teeth and visiting the dentist can help protect your teeth from cavities and other problems.

This girl is testing her blood sugar with a glucose monitor. Most people with diabetes have to test their blood sugar at least once a day.

can cause problems with our teeth, such as **cavities**. Drinking and eating too much extra sugar can also cause **diabetes**, an illness in which a person's body cannot take in sugar and starch normally.

FAST-FOOD FACTS

Most doctors say you should drink at least eight glasses of water a day to stay healthy. If you are very active or play sports, you may need to drink more!

Many Different Choices

There are a lot of good drink choices. Water is the best thing to drink. Our bodies need water to survive. There are many ways to give water some flavor in a healthy way. Try putting lemon or lime slices in water to give it a fruity taste. Some people even put strawberries or cucumbers in their water!

You can check the label on your fruit juice to see if it has any added sugars. Look for kinds that say they are 100 percent juice.

When you are exercising or playing sports, your body loses water when you sweat. That is why it is important to drink a lot of water to replace what you lose.

Milk is another good choice. Milk has calcium, which helps keep bones strong. Fruit drinks, like lemonade or apple juice, can be a good choice sometimes. Fruit drinks usually have a lot of vitamins and nutrients. They can also have a lot of sugar, though.

FAST-FOOD FACTS

As you may guess, low-fat milk has less fat than regular milk. Milk with no fat is called skim milk. The fat has been removed, or skimmed!

Super Choices

Staying healthy means making smart choices every day about the things you eat and drink. Soda can be part of a healthy diet if you have it only once in a while. When you make good drink choices, you are taking care of your body.

In some towns, there are no longer soda machines in schools. Schools want to help kids make healthy choices during the day. Drinking water or low-fat milk with your lunch is always a good choice!

This boy is drinking a glass of milk. Drinking milk with your lunch is an easy way to get some of the vitamins and nutrients you need to stay healthy.

Glossary

artificial (ar-tih-FIH-shul) Made by people, not nature.

calories (KA-luh-reez) Amounts of food that the body uses to keep working.

carbonated (KAHR-buh-nayt-ed) Combined with carbon dioxide.

carbon dioxide (KAHR-bun dy-OK-syd) An odorless, colorless gas. People breathe out carbon dioxide.

cavities (KA-vih-teez) Holes in teeth where they have decayed.

diabetes (dy-uh-BEE-teez) A sickness in which a person's body cannot take in sugar and starch normally.

high-fructose corn syrup (HY-fruk-tohs KAWRN SUR-up) A type of sweetener made from corn in which some of the glucose has been converted into fructose to make it sweeter.

ingredients (in-GREE-dee-unts) The different things that go into food and drinks.

mineral water (MIN-rul WAH-ter) Water that contains natural matter that is not an animal, a plant, or another living thing.

nutrients (NOO-tree-ents) Food that a living thing needs to live and grow.

sweeteners (SWEET-nerz) Substances that make things taste sweeter.

syrups (SUR-ups) Thick, sticky liquids made of sugar and water and often a flavor.

vitamins (VY-tuh-minz) Nutrients that help the body fight illness and grow strong.

Index

Web Sites

Due to the changing nature of Internet links, PowerKids Press has developed an online list of Web sites related to the subject of this book. This site is updated regularly. Please use this link to access the list:

www.powerkidslinks.com/food/soda/